before you

how I dream of entering your mind
dancing with your soul
leaving all else behind

how I wish to consume you
to not only hold
your body
but to have it forever within
my touch
to have your skin as
my skin
your eyes as
my sight
your sleep as
my dreams

let me crawl inside your mind
and find comfort
in its cluttered corners
let me cradle your heart
and trace the scars embedded
in its walls
let me run to where your soul
is hiding
and take its sorrows
to bed

lace your fingers through mine
my soul yearns to know
the secrets of your
mind

my heartbeat pulses
behind my
eyelids
my eyes roam
helplessly in the dark
but I dare not
open them
for you might catch a glimpse
of the fire
burning in my soul

in the few moments
that your defences drop
I see your tender heart
before
pain encased it
and it sings my
name

let me place my lips to
your neck
feel the pulse of your heartbeat
under my mouth
how I wish it beat
for me

you

I desire you as though
I was born
with your name etched
in my bones

how blessed I am to live in your lifetime
to have seen the depths
of your indescribable soul
and kissed your mouth
so pure
I could spend each moment of this life
with you
and still long for you after death

committing my mouth
to the shape of
yours
I pray that your lips
will never know
another

the sun is of no concern to me
you hold me
in time and space

oh how I wish I could
slip into your skin
for holding you in my arms
will never
be close enough

I am bound to you
with ropes of your
touch

dive deep into
the waves of my mind
and let the tide of my thoughts
spell my love
for you

if your mind knew the tale
your lips told
maybe you wouldn't kiss me
like that

you play my heart on its strings
with your expert fingers
you are the puppeteer
and still I stay
until your show ends

I could have left when you said
you had nothing to give
but I chose the heartbreak
for a few moments more in
your embrace
all this in hope
that you'd change
your mind

let me treasure this moment
savour the rich tenderness of
your presence
before you gather your things
and depart
our time forever past

you keep my heart
just within reach
for the nights
you feel alone
as if the longing that consumes
my days
is of no bother to you
how can you be so
heartless?

before you leave
let me know
your soul is mine
for it will kill me to
discover
that as I soothed my restless
heart
with news of your return
you gave your mind to
another

his words were cold and distant
but his hands
they spoke tales of love

I am in no doubt
of what you are
but there is such exhilaration
in loving
a monster

your love sways like the seasons
but I stay
through the wind
and rain
all for the days
we bloom together

if you must give
your body to
another
save your soul
for me

your face exquisite
your eyes kind
but your soul is what
enchants
my mind

my soul entwined with his
having always searched
for the fire
his presence
brings

I was heightened to
his every
movement
he was the sun
and I was rendered
helpless
in his orbit

you slipped under my skin
like a raindrop meeting
the sea
now every fibre of my being
is drowning
in you

though you may be
distant
and indifferent
my soul comes home to you

your touch ignited a spark
which had lay dormant in
my mind
and it continues to burn
knowing nothing of sleep
or fear
only of you
and the fire you bring

your touch like electricity
to my skin
your words like a caress
to my soul

I trace the soft lines
of your chest
committing every feature
to memory
for the days we are apart
thoughts of you will be
my only solace

my face cradled
in the small of your neck
intoxicated by the scent
of your skin
the gentle beating
of your heart
let my love
entice you to sleep

I will encase my hands around
yours
as you hold your heart
and wait
wait until your trust builds
and your grip loosens
until I caress your heart
in my hands
until every memory of pain
has been replaced with one
of love

ours is a tale of fate
and love
as tragic is it is
passionate

I feel distance in your
touch
as though your fingers
are leaving the imprints
of a man
already departed

the warmth of your touch
seeps into my skin
and saturates my bones

you say I ask
too much of you
but how hard it is
to lower my expectations
when you embody
all I desire

I romanticised each word
you uttered
until you became
all I'd dreamed of
and I loved deeply
as it broke my heart

he held me
in an embrace that my foolish mind
could conceive only
as love
as he whispered
his words
of departure

my body is numb to all
but the heat
of your breath against my neck
the pressure
of your hand on my thigh
the sweet lies
you whisper
invading my senses

you are as though I have found
what had always been absent
for at last
I do not need a body
or a drug
to feel something

the dark beings that lurk
within the confines
of my mind
are stilled
in his presence
and I am
at peace

he caressed the shards
of my being
his tender hands
spoke nothing
of the brokenness
that lay beneath them
my mind willingly
undressed
to the depths
of its vulnerability
for my scars
had found salvation
in his
presence

intimacy
is the closest thing we have
to heaven
and heartbreak
to hell

allow this love to drive you
to the brink of insanity
for only then will you feel
the moon
on your skin and
the sun
in your veins

I fell hopelessly into
the clutches of love
for in its madness
I found
humanity

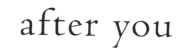

how foolish I was
to believe your touch
held something more than
desire
how naïve to entangle
your lust with my
love

I awake
to yet another unfamiliar arm
draped over me
how many lovers
will it take to uncloud
my mind
how many bodies
must I hold before I stop
feeling you

you left me broken
at your will
be still my heart
be still

I will survive
without you
my days may be
long
my chest may be
heavy
but I shall go on
living

each beat of my heart is
laced with loss
every corner of my mind is
tainted with
you

each day is a
little less without you
and soon they'll be
but a way to pass the time

I knew the pain would come
and yet
I couldn't drag myself from
your presence
I held you close in
ignorant bliss
until your eyes fell upon
the likes of another
so now
as my heart breaks
in my chest
I can do little but weep at my
self-induced
heartache

how many lips must I kiss
until your taste
no longer
haunts
my tongue?

I immersed myself completely
in you
now I must unearth myself
again

I am curious as to what
damaged you so
badly
and left you with such a
tainted perception of
reality

as you lay with yet another
lover
your heart cold
and your mind alone
you will be haunted with thoughts
of how
I loved you
and how
you broke my heart to shield
yours

lay in the empty caress of another
discover that countless
hollow lovers
cannot heal
your heart

I was foolish
to believe you'd ever choose
love over lust
the desire that engulfs your mind
knows only
the language of touch

you hide
behind the shadows of
your heartbreak
as if it permits you
to be so cruel

I cannot bear to watch you
with her
to see you place those lips upon
her mouth
lips that once spoke volumes
of your love
for me

I weep as if each tear is a
footstep
running me back
to you

you'll wake with a soul
aching of loss
for you have discovered
that my doting heart
will wait
no longer

each thought that
graces my mind
is tainted
with being without
you

how can you walk
from the wreckage of our romance
unscathed?
as my soul
lays in pieces
amongst the shards of
our love

you ask why I will not
change my ways
for you
but you don't dare see
I must continue to love myself
long after
you have gone

how do I grieve
over a love I never had
to lose?
a man who was never mine
to hold?

I think of you
as I lay beside
my lover of tonight
as he filled my body
the vacancy in my soul
grew
will lust ever conquer
my need for
you?

I was engulfed with the
loss of you
my mind could not
comprehend
but as the tears rain on
my tender cheeks
my soul
begins to mend

the tears and the pain
over and over
again
now I sit
blood tainted black
weeping for the essence
of my soul
long left

how I had longed
to be the woman you cherished
the woman deemed worthy
of committing to
but in a moment of clarity
I saw perhaps
it was you
that did not deserve
me

from your hungry lips
my mouth travelled south
to kiss upon your delicate
neck
to feel your pulse
quicken
beneath my touch
oh how I wished to
end it

you give your soul
to mend others hearts
but they only notice your scars
and
depart

I gave you my heart
there is no more of me
left to give

it was as though in your
departure
you took every emotion I had
with you
and left a shell of a girl
with a
heartbeat

let me bathe in this
delicious despair
soak in your lies
like a fish
to sea

as your tongue touches
mine
do you taste the words
I wasted on
you?

your mouth was new as
I kissed it
you were no longer the man
I'd loved
and I no longer
the tragic lover who had
cherished your touch
times before

I looked into his
heart
and a vacant expression
greeted me

let me pour every pain
into the words
upon these pages
so that I may feel
a heartbeat
against my chest
again

time and time again
I wonder
is it strength or
foolishness
to be found in the pursuit
of an unreciprocated
love?

memories of your touch
haunt me
I pray for the time
when I no longer crave
your breath
against my
neck

me

I am more than a body for
your exploration
I am a mind
once opened
a heart
once broken
a soul
once loved

I long to be the woman I was
before
you broke my heart
a woman
unexamined and unrecorded
with a soul
so softened with innocence
that it believed
in a love
everlasting

I long to
give
but I am only
taken
I desire to be
known
but I show you only
my body

I am drawn
by an ancient desire
sustaining the belief in a
love that saves

finding sanctuary in each man I believe
to love
but he only gives
name to the nameless

he is not my purpose
nor is he a solution

he is but a mere man
that I look to fill a void
long diminished

the state they leave your
heart in
that is enough to answer
any controversy
in your soul

keep your heart soft
so soft
it cannot be broken
so soft
it cannot be claimed

I lurk amongst a sea of
lovers
hungry for a touch to
make me feel alive

the familiar wave of senselessness
washes over me
and I sit
drowning in a sea
of my own
discontent

do I hunt for love
all to bask in the pain
that comes in
heartbreak?

for in those moments
there is an intensity
which replaces the
constant state of
numbness
which engulfs my
mind

say your sweet nothings
and you can have
my body
but I'll save my soul
for me

as you grip my thighs
my mind will wander
to a time when they were cherished

as you bite my neck
I will dream of the gentle kisses
once laid there

I fall willingly into the greedy grasp
of lust
but will I ever
allow the gentle fingers of love
to again
stroke my cheek?

may my tender heart be
forever vulnerable
to the ploy
that is love

I hungrily prowl the streets of
the city
hunting for acceptance
like a beggar for a meal

my soul belonging both
everywhere
and nowhere
all at once

why is it that when I am
alone
loneliness engulfs me so?
whispers sweet nothings in
my ear
like there is no love
in this world
for me

I become numb to my emotions
and my surroundings
as I plummet into the haze
that occupies
my mind
like a cloud blocking
the sun
my mind too has become hidden
in the shade
of my mental
preoccupations

I watch in jealousy
as the lovers kiss
and the children play
how does happiness come
with such ease
to them?

how challenging it is
to love oneself
when it is though
my body
is all I have to
offer

why must I meet them
when they are
broken
to pour my soul into
fixing theirs
all to be left for someone
worthy
of their healed selves

it is as though I am
on a raft
drifting slowly out
to sea

I wish to paddle my hands in
the water
to return to the island
of the living
but my body remains still

I can do little
but watch
as the distance between myself
and sanity
grows